# *the City Fox and others in our community*

**the complete collection**

Chris Parker

Chiselbury

Published by Chiselbury Publishing, a division of Woodstock Leasor Limited, 14 Devonia Road, London N1 8JH, United Kingdom

www.chiselbury.com

ISBN: 978-1-916556-06-5

# the City Fox

**others:**

not the ones already mentioned, but different ones.

*'We learn through community*
*- even when alone.'*
Epiah Khan

## In the city

Many years ago, I said to my teacher, 'I truly respect those people who are so dedicated they leave everything behind to go in search of themselves and their God.'

He replied, 'So do I. However, I respect even more those who do the same thing whilst remaining in the city. You see, in the roar of the city worlds collide. They jar against each other. Connections are hidden behind man-made distractions that seek to fill our minds. It is easy to become lost.'

Then he led me on a walk through busy streets.

He didn't speak to me again for more than a year.

My teacher continues to live in the city.

## Writer

I wake early.
Every home in the street is in darkness,
my wife softened on our bed,
the air in other rooms untouched.
I have no idea of the words,
only a need, overwhelming even sleep, to sit at this desk,
shadowed by my favourite lamp,
to roll between my fingers the ink pen that no one else must use.

Desperate, I take a breath meaning to use it
and as I struggle with the inevitable gap
a bird sings in the coldness of the garden.
Just a bird I never see
singing to no one in particular,
singing from its heart
because it has to.

How can a bird do so easily the thing I find most difficult?
Why is my pen so distant?

## Learning language

Bun bu ichi
the Japanese phrase
speaks of the two great powers,
the pen and the sword,
by which we shape our world.

At least the sword
beautiful and balanced
which can kill in less than an instant
is forged in fire,
its edge so sharp it barely exists.

This is pure transformation.

Dullness stretched and cultured
into a tool, a symbol, an artist's gift.
Its creator, drenched in sweat,
honoured for his sacrifice,
keeping hands close to nature, breath hissing into the flames.

If only our words were crafted in such a way,
could serve such purpose,
reflect such commitment.

Instead our word-swords wound by accident.
- cutting ourselves, you understand, as well as others -
running amok with sound
and shape.

Perhaps one day a swordsmith will teach children how to
shape their words,
brighten their senses,
sharpen their silence.

## Gardener

When nature makes a decision
there's no going back.
She keeps her silence,
letting the birds and the flowers
the wind and the ice
speak on her behalf.

When nature makes a decision
She is teaching us.

## Gardener (ii)

Nature is no timekeeper.

The leaf doesn't fall when it does because time is money.
The bud doesn't open to maintain this week's schedule.
Nature doesn't count the seasons because they are her.

Nature has no plan.

She left that to us.

## Hunter

When is the beginning?

Does the hunt start when the prey is sensed,
or with the first pangs of hunger?

Or is it further back
at birth
or even before?

Does it begin with a question
or with desire?

Is the hunt
part of the hunter
like a limb or an organ?
Or is it just a behaviour
as necessary as breath?

And when does it end?
Is it with the kill, the feed, or the transference into energy?

Is our ability to ask these questions
the source of our power
or the cause of our limitation?

Can a hunter have an intellect?

## Mary & Peter

They were the best of friends.
The very best.
Since the sacred oath taken on the day when
they were just more than children and
just less than the promise of the morning sun,
- before their first lover and long before their first loss,
before they began counting time through the growth of
others,
before either knew what it really meant -
they pledged a lifetime of friendship.
The very best.
Even partners said, 'Those two have no secrets.'

Yet so often it would wake him in the night,
tugging him from sleep,
to wonder in silence how it might have been.

And for all his life he knew the smell of her.

## Summer clouds

The cloud factory, standing next to the black-as-coal road
that twists and winds its way like a frozen river,
spews out grey, venomous clouds that threaten harm and
dampen spirits.

I've heard it said they've closed the factories that make
summer clouds.

## Priest

*secret notes*

When I wake in the morning the first thing I turn to
in this wondrous world
is
Me.
The things my body needs,
the race my mind insists upon,
the fears my ego-self creates for the coming day.

With the answers all around me
I choose instead to go inwards,
stopping short of the sacred place.

## Soldier

*back from Afghanistan*

I'm rushing towards a future of my own creation, all of it
bleak.

What part of me feels the need to ignore the bright emptiness
of the space ahead and see only darkness?
What part of me returns to this endlessly when I walk
through the city?
Why do I hurt myself?

Today I walked through a thousand lives.
Each as precious as mine.
Perhaps
a woman trembling at the promise of a new career,
a man praying silently for an ailing friend,
a couple who had just made love,
a mother missing her children for an afternoon,
a teacher light with his sharing.

I didn't see one of them.

I know they didn't see me.

## Charity worker

I have never been able to give without needing something in return.
Most of all I seek the joy of giving unexpectedly and freely,
of watching it ripple through the mind and body of another.

Oh, my false heart!

Researchers say *Because* is a powerful word.
It promises reasons and justifications
offers explanations and understanding.
It is the link between cause and effect.
It is the life-blood of the Scientist.

I understand *Because.*
Sometimes it is part of my disguise.
Sometimes it is my apology.
It is always the reason for my giving.

The God I believe in knows everything apart from this word.

## The city fox

The city fox shares everything she has with her family.
She teaches by her example how to survive in the grey forest.

From her the cubs learn how to make any place their home,
how to avoid distraction.
They learn the value of invisibility,
the power that comes from weakness,
how to live in the shadows.

The darkness is no place for adaptation or creativity.
Around the waste of human existence there is no need for
imagination or expectation.
In the hedgerow and the garden bushes
the waste ground and the playing fields,
just the keenest nose and the sharpest hearing
bring reward:
another day in hiding
another night to hunt.

## The old man

Some people say that the old man at 102 is a mystic
who retired early to dedicate himself to prayer.
They say that he speaks in tongues
and dances in his garden to the music of the angels.

Some people say that the old man is mad
because
he is always happy,
even though he knows they have closed the factories that
make summer clouds.

## Dog walker

How curious and excited
the spaniel
racing and twisting by the canal for the second time in the day,
empty and open
joyous
and
timeless.

Trembling
she rushes,
travelling on her breath
every difference a new world.

One
and
one
and
one.

All else forgotten.

## Soldier (ii)

Sometimes Death touches,
fills me briefly
in my gut and mind
and so many thoughts press
heavy and cold
that I hear none of them.

Where am I?

Sometimes
- these very different times -
Death strokes the fear my mind creates
and I cry at the freedom in its promise.

Who am I?

## Influence

We came into this world
not because we had a plan
but because someone else did.

We came into this world
knowing only how to play and learn,
how to be grateful,
curious
and brave.

Who taught us to change?

## So much in one minute

My grandson is learning the hardest of things.
Dragging himself upright he takes
faltering steps
towards inevitable collapse;
with tears varnishing his cheeks
he reaches for his mother
his cries dissolving at her touch,
ready in a heartbeat to start again
as if nothing bad had happened.

## Soldier (iii)

I am so trammeled up with fear
I cannot think about what comes next.

I will not meet my final death this way.

## Mary & Peter (ii)

She spoke with her back turned to him
in the coldness of their bed
in the darkness of their room.

She could not speak of loneliness or fear
not now
when she had to be so precise
not now
with her back turned as a warning sign.
Instead she told him of her anger and disappointment,
her investment going unrewarded.

With her back serving as a barrier
she looked forward, blinking occasionally,
into the darkness.

## Priest (ii)

*on counselling*

Oh! To be able to see so clearly that we understand another
by reading the lines on their face,
by watching the movements of their fingertips,
by the glance of their eyes.
To listen so acutely that we hear the voices of their past or
their fears for the future
through their words in the present.
To be so interested that our senses tingle at every opportunity
to know them better.

Or, instead, to stay imprisoned in our own body,
warded by our own thoughts?

## The old man (ii)

'Why not just give yourself up to the inevitability of success?'
The old man at 102 spoke to me suddenly as we queued in
our local supermarket.

'Why not just give yourself up to the inevitability of success
the way a cat
gives herself up
to the stone floor
in the heat
of the summer sun?

'After all, everyone becomes great at something.
It can be eating, or smoking, or fear.
It can be doubt or denial.
It can be lack of awareness.
So why not make it giving
in all its many forms?
Why not make it joy?
Why not just surrender to the stone?

'Aah! I must stop now.
Look - it's your turn to pay.'

## Measurement

'You must do your best,'
the schoolteacher said.

The boy's eyes widened
and because he had not yet been taught about percentages,
did not yet understand the importance of exams,
was ignorant of measurements and systems
and instead knew
only
how to be curious
he asked,
'How will I know ever know when I have done my best?

## Schoolteacher

I hurt too easily
when
others
do not behave how I expect them to,
when
the weather
is not as I hoped,
when
results
do not go my way.

Yet
rarely do I meet my own expectations;
rarely am I the person
I believe in.

And still there are people who love me.

## Wrapping

My grandson plays with the paper rather than the gift.
He slaps it with his palms.
He pulls and tumbles backwards.
He tears and scrunches
and oh so quickly favours another piece.

His parents watch, taking photos with their iPhones,
comfortable and proud,
secure in their new build,
on hand when the wrapping proves too much.

**Martin**

*alone*

I have made a business of my life,
played my part in creating a city of expectation.
(Although I show my weakness often by claiming it the work of others.)

I could have learned from the city fox
comfortable in the shadows,
from the branch bending gladly this way and that,
from the spaniel forgetful and joyous.

I could have blessed the flower for offering its delicate face full to the heavens.
I could have found release in loss,
swopped every agenda for just a little more awareness.

I could have been led by the seasons and not by the clock,
thought less about winning and more about service,
created words on the forge of curiosity and in the fire of love,
celebrated without an audience
like a bird singing in the chill of the early morning.

I could have…

Only I was too busy making a business of my life, you see
and now I fear it is too late;
I am so much the creation of my own habits.

Although - wait! -
I hear the city fox
whispering,
'Human! Listen!
There is always time for rebirth.

This alone is nature's business.
The universe is all around you.
Always.
You are still small enough to grow!'

And I believe her - I have to -
my hope,
the city fox.

## Newsagent

*closing down*

It's snowing
again.
Cold, freezing winds
blowing all the way from the Arctic.
Roads closed.
Train lines down.
The city stilled by the worst winter for twenty years.

It doesn't matter that they can't walk to me in this.
Truth is, they don't need me now that news is 24/7
when everything is only one click away
when you can see everything
show everything
comment on everything
protected by a password and the screen of entitlement
supported by friends and followers you have never met
and never will
joined by the frostbite of technology numbing our senses
blackening our reach.

Truth is, this is how it always ends
closing the door for the last time
one click
empty and quiet.
Frozen.

## Pavement clues

The residue of a thought
clings
like snow to a pavement;
sometimes it hardens, thickens,
becoming treacherous;
sometimes it dissolves in unexpected heat.

The residue of a thought
there
beneath our footprint.

## **Occasional farm boy**

*lost outside the city*

Invest in loss, the sage advised.
Care enough to be curious.
Love enough to risk.
Create hope.

Only that was then and this is now.
Only *plus ça change, plus c'est la même chose.*
Only it cannot have been the same for a man finding wisdom walking a continent barefoot.
Only why should planes, trains and brogues make such a difference?

---

There was a time when I was not yet turned ten
when my uncle left me with strict instructions to keep hold of both dogs
no matter what.
They tugged after him as he strode towards the barn where the birth was going badly wrong.

The dogs, mother and son, looked at me
wildness in their eyes
as my uncle disappeared from view.

They tugged again.

The mother, Sally,
- how crazy that a name should sound so harmless
and yet the mouth seem so threatening -
the mother, Sally, jumped against me.
I staggered back

almost losing my grip on the leash.

This next time they jumped together
their claws scratching my chest, their spittle flying into my face.

The fragile command that shook itself free from my throat
was more a plea for understanding than a demand for peace.
The mother, the wiser of the two, dropped low, nipping at my ankles,
as her son tried again to force his face into mine.

My hand opened,
releasing dogs and shame and fear in the same split-second.

The dogs raced into the barn.
The shame and fear stayed close,
squeezing out tears
crushing my chest.

The cow bellowed. The dogs barked. The men's raised voices were filled with anger.

This was the first time my imagination broke free,
running wild
to create the worst of all possible worlds.

My uncle brought it back under control
ten minutes later
returning from the barn with dogs at heel.
His brogues were muddied
there was blood, too.

'Saved them both,' he said. 'Just.'

He took a long, deep breath. 'Next time,' he glanced at the dogs who sat immediately.
'Next time, keep hold.
Understand?'

---

The sage wrote, 'The only thing between yourself and the universe is your skin. You are closer to freedom than you think.'

---

Perhaps it was different then?

## Writer (ii)

We travelled far from home to find relaxation,
to create distance from something we define, casually, as the pressure of the city.
We travelled, I guess, in search of peace.

Of course, we stressed about the selection of clothes, the timings and the paperwork.
We monitored the weather forecasts and the travel information.
We took computers, Sat Nav and phones,
packed adaptors so that everything would fit and be fully charged.

Eventually we found the place with blue sky and greenery,
mountains, fresh water and a different language.

After two (or maybe three) days
the queues and delays
- the frequent confusion of travel -
were forgotten.

On the sixth day I read this poem out loud,
I think it was the sixth day
because
I know that I hadn't yet started thinking about the return journey.
When I finished reading
she said, 'I don't understand it all.
Do you?'

'No,' I replied after some delay, 'I am only the writer.'

I wished, later, that I had said, 'They are only words.

I just happened to hear them first.'

I wish, most of all, that I could structure my thoughts without a constant reference to myself.
Perhaps then I wouldn't need to travel so far.

## Mary & Peter (iii)

And in the night
with her back turned to him
with her change in breathing telling him that she was far away,
that she was lost in her cold emotion,
he chose to wait
and listen
in silence.

At least he said no words out loud.
He offered no contradiction or promise,
no suggestion of warmth.

How could he reach out to her?
Trapped by his choice to make this life enough,
to accept,
rather than start again.

## Newsagent (ii)

*on reflection*

Everything turns full circle.
That is the headline of my life.

I looked into the mirror this morning and saw my father
looking back.
Not the young, muscular version
but rather the old man
with sag and loss
with jowl and bag
with blurry eyes filmed with images of the past
the future closer
the question *why?*
long since replaced
by the question
*when?*

I looked into the mirror this morning
and shaved a man I thought was gone.

## The city fox (ii)

*answering the question*

The fox hunts without distraction as the city whirls around her,
neon signs flashing characters and invitations
cars racing between gears and lights
urgency, wrapped in design, screaming at the night sky
turning the city ever-inward.

Yet the fox hunts without distraction.
She has her purpose,
given irrepressible priority by her young, left behind,
her nature
more compelling than any fashion.

Her nose flares and twitches
her eyes penetrate the shades of darkness,
her pads trace a line set by only the most pertinent cues.

She kills silently, teeth piercing skin and crushing bone
without warning or posture or thought.
She has no conscience.
She never has, and never will, fear consequence.
There is no separation between what she does and who she is.

Best then, if to die at all, to be killed by the city fox.

## Bank manager

The man was sitting on a piece of damp cardboard, legs
crossed as if in meditation, with his back to the wall of the
bank, presenting both a challenge and a plea.
At least that was my perception. I never thought to ask for
his.

'Spare a pound,' he said, as I keyed in my number.
'Why just a pound?'
'The thing I've learnt,' he said, 'is that everything begins
before it begins and ends after it ends. Perhaps if I'd learnt
that sooner…'

He knew the price of a bed in the nearest hostel.
(I asked him as if that had always been my intention.)
When I gave the money I saw fear in his eyes.
'Move on,'
I said firmly,
as if we had struck a deal.

## Gardener (iii)

Silence is born in the moment when night meets morning,
when nature passes from one to the other
when the city fox has disappeared,
before the first bird sings.

It‘s a silence filled with certainty
that can only be felt when there are no more questions to be asked
no more possibilities to be explored.

It’s the silence that exists beyond division;
when the decision has been made.

## The old man (iii)

The old man at 102 has died.

He slipped on the damp grass dancing to the music of the angels.
He broke his hip
survived the operation
then lost his breath
to
complications.

They say that the old man died with a smile on his face,
as if he had heard the answer to a question,
as if he was looking past the grey, venomous clouds.

They say he died
knowing that it was part of a process.

I wish I knew.

## Writer (iii)

If my pen had a life of its own
would the words run free,
celebrating their escape from the shackles of my mind?

Or would they stumble and shiver,
creeping huddled across the lines of a page
they have never seen before?

Would I recognise them?

Are they my prisoner
or am I theirs?

If my pen had a life of its own
could it answer this?

## Travellers

My friend died on Wednesday at 6am.

In a city thousands of miles away it was another time
altogether.
There, in that same split-second,
other lives ended;
lives I will never know.

If reality exists on this earth
perhaps it is somewhere in the space between two people;
the emptiness we fill.

## Cat

The cat pads instinctively into the spotlight
dissolving down onto the warmth of the stone;
a silk cloth settling over the curves of the uneven floor.

Her eyes close in immediate submission and, at once,
everything is hidden
the stillness broken only by her belly, pulsing gently.

This is not performance,
this is life so filled to the brim
there is no space for choice.
She does not need to twist and turn to find her comfort,
she does not wonder if she ought to rest,
she has never questioned her identity or her potential.
She has no options,
she can be nothing else,
just a perfect cat
giving
herself
to the Earth.

**Breath**

Without the cultivation of appropriate resources
even the greatest plan, the most inspiring vision, the worthiest intention,
is doomed to failure.
This is what the business guru means when he says,
'The gap between imagination and success is crossed only on the bridge of resource.'

It is a bridge, he writes, that becomes both the symbol and the measure of success.
It is a bridge redefined and rebuilt as success grows.

'Power,' the guru says, 'Is the ability to cultivate, combine and direct resource.
Power is far more than money, or networks, than equipment, staffing or skills,
although these are all a part of it.

Power is the ability to summon and prioritise, to transform the ordinary into the extraordinary, to create and manage momentum as no other can.
Power and the symbols of power are all resource dependent.'

So he teaches, through workshops and seminars, through books and online.
People flock to him from across the world.
Even in his own land he is a prophet, a visionary, who proves his truth through his own example.

And, because he is a guru of business and only that,
in all his teaching about power and resource
he never mentions breath.
Not once.

## Schoolteacher (ii)

The pub was crowded.
Friday teatime,
standing room only in no-man's land.

The schoolteacher saw me look.
Somehow
even though he was on the other side of the bar
even though he was lost in thought
even though it was only a glance.

Eyes in the back of his head
I thought.
Teacher-vision.

He raised his glass to me
barely, just a syllable of movement,
his smile even less.

'I'm tired,' the smile said,
'tired of the responsibility of talking
of the weight of listening
of the endless measurements.
Please don't look at me.
It hurts.'

## Travellers (ii)

The bee was full and fat and bold in colour,
it's wings a measure of excitement and joy
that,
I suspect,
I cannot even imagine.

Somehow,
even though she was giving every drop of her attention to the flower
- or, perhaps, for that very reason -
she spurred a question in my mind,
translated in an instant so that I could
if I chose
be grateful and curious and dip in to its offering,
its far less obvious learning.

And have you ever,
the question asked,
forged a route
rather than simply followed one

do you know how it feels for your footprints to be the first,
to not know what lies ahead
and yet press on?

The question, *Are you an Explorer?*
is
of course
a question about Education,
that process of discovery and development
far removed from the need for clear endings and right
answers and the rush to raise hands into the air.

The question, 'Are you an Explorer?'
asks
how comfortable you are with not knowing,
how free you are from the prison of comparison,
how far-reaching is your home?

There are always Explorers walking amongst us,
waiting patiently,
like all great destinations,
to be discovered.

## Bird

*the gardener explains how*

There is only one chance to make a
first impression;
that is what the experts teach.

Those experts in communication
who know how to structure and sequence,
combine information and emotion,
demand attention.

In the garden the bird's feathers ruffle against
the early morning chill;
she settles quickly
balancing on the pencil-thin branch.

Here, now, she's drawn to the opportunity of the new day
the openness
the pure space.
It draws the song from her.

She doesn't see the pen
stilled by her voice,
nor the jealous hand.

## Jean

When Jean was eight years old she dreamed of being a princess.

When she was thirteen
she imagined being a pop star.

When she was sixteen
she prayed she wasn't pregnant.

Now - and Jean would never have guessed this -
she works in the petrol station
and sometimes she sells condoms.

She makes sense of it all.

Her sleeplessness is not caused by her life,
rather by the fact that she does not know how to sell dreams
to her daughter.

## Wrapping (ii)

'Once,' Jean said
after too many glasses of Pinot Grigio,
after Time had been called without any sense of invitation or request,
'Once,' Jean said, 'I gave my heart completely.
Silly me,
I chose the wrong words to go with it.'

## Syd

In moments of what we would call clarity,
that he might call 'lamp' or 'zoo'
or any other words his damaged brain
and forceful mouth
combined to construct,
Syd recognised what we might call his irreversible loss,
his change,
his irreparable damage.

In moments of what we would call clarity,
he tried to kill himself.
Those moments stretched by his determination.

The neighbours and the shopkeepers who knew him before
the stroke
did their best to accommodate him.
'It's such a shame,' they said.
'He was so lovely.'

Towards the end
he wore shorts
even when the weather bit,
his legs stick thin
the muscles wasted.

We never said that his mind and emotion – to be more
precise, his emotional control – were wasted,
we never said that.
We were more like the neighbours and the others,
more likely to say how sorry we were
without ever having the courage to consider who we felt most
sorry for.

I doubt we had more moments of clarity than he.

The second stroke took him like a tidal wave;
washed everything away but the shell.

At his funeral I performed the words I had written and practised.
I did a good job, they said.
It seemed to help.

## Me

I have more skin now than when I began,
but the wrinkles are returning,
along with the excess.

My friends say, kindly, that my skin has character;
a face showing a life lived.
I know only how difficult it is to write a new story
on a crumpled sheet.

On the day my father died,
asleep,
his skin became unexpectedly smooth; creases that had been
deepening disappeared below the surface;
a warm pink glazed his cheeks.

If you have ever seen the sun setting
-drifting colours from beyond the horizon-
above a calm sea that was violent only hours before,
you will know exactly what I mean.

Sometimes I feel comfortable within my skin.
Sometimes I am removed from it, as if distanced by a lens.
Sometimes I look at the heavens,
feel my heels balanced on the spinning earth,
and something I cannot quite remember makes me smile.

## E.K?

I met Epiah Khan yesterday outside the bakery.
At least, that was how he introduced himself,
as if he knew his name would mean something.

'Man decorates the world', he said without preamble,
'man decorates the world through the strength of his will and
the flatulence of his ego.
Remember, knowing is not the same as being.'

Then he offered me a doughnut.

## Sam's lesson

I had a dog, Sam,
a squat, red, cheerful fellow
with a wide, easy grin that stretched forever across muscular cheeks.

He growled at me once, as a young adult still testing his place,
his head low over his food,
his tongue flicking out, curling over exposed teeth as if tasting the air between us.

Fortunately this was so unexpected I had no time to think
- it was the lesson he taught me about instinct buried just below the surface.

My hands turned him, one swift precise motion, onto his back
cupping the underside of his jaw
exposing the softness of his throat
lowering my face over it.

We stayed that way for some time
seconds
stretching into a lifelong understanding.

Often, after that, whenever he felt the need to press me for affection
he would roll over demanding his belly to be rubbed,
sharing the pulse in his throat without hesitation.

I found it all but impossible to resist.

Always, after that, I hugged my friends
clear in the realisation that we place our open throats against
each other's collar;
a sign of trust more significant than the brief touch of hands
or even lips on skin.

Once, after that, I met a woman who closed the gap so
completely
I offered her my throat without question or doubt.

She took it.

Then offered me her own.

## Bird (ii)

The city parks are filled with
people passing through.

Some
listening to music as they run,
planning their day
thoughts faster than their feet.

Those already dressed for work
are slower
no less deliberate
a phone pressed to their ear like a baby to the breast.

Lovers are the slowest,
hips pressing as they walk
talking through the open-mouthed smiles
of shared intimacy
pupils dilated by remembering, imagining
and hope.

In the garden
the bird plunges her beak into the soil,
stabbing down without hesitation.

Withdrawing
her head cocks from side to side
- how stupid to think she is listening!

She stabs again
a staccato attack.

Seconds later
look
– there! –
a worm
disturbed
by her effort.

Bird holds her place in triumph,
having shaken the earth.

## The old man (iv)

They say
that the old man at 102
left a will.
Not that he had any possessions to pass on
nor anyone who knew him
for that matter.

They say
that, in his will,
the old man wrote,

'I leave you the grass in my garden.
I hope that one day you are drawn to dance
barefoot in the early morning
when the grass is still damp from the night's touch,
when the earth is fertile with the new dawn
still as a mother feeding her young.

'I pray that you dance from your heart,
that the earth clings to the soles of your feet.
I pray that you search for the silence behind the noise.'

## Martin (ii)

*connected*

For many years I sought control. Which, of course, is another
way of saying I believed I had the power to create certainty.
(In my defence it is a common illness.)
I wrote and exercised plans. I developed resources. I did
everything I could to shape today and tomorrow. Which took
all of my attention.

So I missed the lessons offered to me:
the branch dancing this way and that on the wind;
the flower's face opening to the heavens, capable only of
receiving;
the city fox, slinking, sleeping close by, never dreaming of the
wild forest
nor missing it.

A wise man saw me once in a dream and said,
'Imagine being a circle with a dot at its centre.
A dot you can barely see and yet a circle, too.
Imagine that is your Self.'

This is how he broke me.

'There is a light', he said, 'that can only be lit by weakness.
It can light a thousand others and is never diminished by its
giving.
It can be a touch, a look, or just a word.'

Once, thank God, as I stood crying
the night sky whispered,
'Nature knows nothing of weakness nor death, of winning nor
losing.'
As the circle opened – just a glimmer I suspect –

my thoughts dissolved
all knowledge and questions forgotten,
all sense of self lost in that great unknowing.
There, in that timeless place beyond separation,
I was the city fox.
And all the rest.

## Network

Network is just another word for association,
which, in turn,
is just another word for connection,
and connections flow into each other
leaving us compelled to create meaning,
which is, it seems, part of our nature,
whether that is the so-called nature of our own creation
or that which precedes and surrounds us
and asks nothing more than we learn how to look.

My career teachers,
whom I called *parent*
knew nothing of this.
Instead of a net working to connect, combine and create
they saw instead a ladder
steep
with steps beyond the reach of their imagination
and therefore of my possibility.

Career is just another word for life
or so it seems for many people,
and life is just another word for opportunity,
which is the result of space and curiosity
acknowledged and combined to a greater or lesser degree.

And that great space cries out for teachers
who cast their net towards it,
freed from the need for legacy,
or the well of justification,
teachers with nothing to prove
other than their willingness to release
and their strength to support.

And network is,
of course,
a word we use too often
too small
because here
- right now -
in this instant
we are all sharing the world together.

This is our time.

## Community centre

One day a city fox braved the edges of the petrol station.
Jean saw him first, in a quiet moment.

He returned the next day.

She named him Basil.
She told her regulars.
They fed him.
The fox became a regular too.
The cycle was established.

People talked.

People
all sorts of people
shared their particular story of the city fox who came to be
fed
at the petrol station.

People
all sorts of people
came to the petrol station in the hope of
seeing him
or
feeding him.

Sometimes they did.

He disappeared abruptly,
presumed dead.

And still they talked.
Even more so, truth be told.

After all, the space needs to be filled.

Beyond the stories, he left his lesson. Which is simply this:
It takes only one city fox to create a community.

Or just something else.

******************

**debris**

**inside and out**

**debris:**

'broken or torn pieces of something larger.'

*'Whatever we do*
*wherever we go*
*we leave things behind*
*- always.'*
Epiah Khan

## The end

'Endings,' my teacher said, 'are really so important. They are important because they are the last things we leave behind. Everything that has gone before is reviewed through the prism of the ending. And the end is always nearer than we think, close as our next footstep.'

In 1978 my teacher left the country suddenly and without warning. I had been studying with him most days for two years. He had made clear his intention to return home sometime in the coming months, but I had expected a farewell meeting and a plan set in place for my continuing education. Instead, it was worse than nothing. His abrupt departure left me feeling as if I had fallen into an unseen hole whilst walking towards an inevitable and unwanted destination.

I never doubted, however, that I would continue my practice. I had gone too far to consider turning back. To strengthen my resolve I clung on to the belief that this was a deliberate test lovingly set, that I hadn't been abandoned despite the silence and the distance. And so the next phase of my study began.

It continued for almost a decade. It ended when I finally made contact with him again; the result of a sustained search filled with more than a few moments of doubt, several dead ends and the occasional near miss. My teacher's reply, a long hand-written letter, offered congratulations and an invitation to visit. Six months later I was in his hometown. We were face to face once more. It was a new beginning.

Another ending followed.

As did, of course, the next beginning.

Over time a circle formed.

## Human remains

Words
like bones
are left behind.

Those laying open to the elements
are kicked, picked and rearranged
used as spikes or signposts
turned into intellectual playthings and pathways
bounced between ever-expanding possibilities
or threaded into an already over-ripe perspective.

Others sink below the surface
reaching the deepest strata
settling there
creating over time
layers of certainty
solid as prison walls
necessary as air.

The most powerful few,
rare, well-crafted shapes
offering both foundation and fortune,
become the rich vein of passion and fortitude.

Words
like bones
are left behind;
easy to forget
in the swill of sound.

## If the Devil exists

A fifty-year-old explains:

If the devil exists
he's in my brain
or at least his one trick is
seeded somehow into my neurons

one trick
so easy to do
so natural
there's no practice needed
that's the devilish part.

Let me tell you:

I can hold opportunity in my hand
show it up-close to those around
wait until they, too, feel its immediacy and promise cast a shadow
and then
in the blink of that darkness
I make it go
disappearing so completely
neither I
nor they
ever know whose pocket, eyeline or dream
it will appear in next.

I can take the biggest, brightest lessons
- the beetle and the bee
the curious tree bark
the uncut grass
the ten million others -

and hide their inspiration
completely
behind a career path
or the lie of security
or two great holidays a year.

I can spin hope between my fingers
and dissolve it into thin air
vanish trust behind a speck of fear
gratitude behind the smallest change.

Yet my trick
for all its power
earns neither kudos nor concern,
disguised so well as the common experience.

## The
## old man at 102
## looking down

Every crack in the pavement
is the signature-mix of our lives

proof we
exist
move
share
grow
create
change
die
    exist

every pavement crack is just a chance
to trip
ignore
remember
                anything we choose.

## Train driver

Drawn underground by the pull of time saved
the certainty of the crowd
the comfort of unthinking habit

footsteps merging, slowing, shortening
breath doing the same
eyes fixed ahead

following the tunnel
taking the stairs
the hypnotist's irresistible persuasion
going down
deeper
          and
                    deeper
without even knowing

down to an agreed unspoken crowding
the pressing and sweat of social proof

our journey shared
passed on
unquestioned

the way it is.

Please
mind the gap between the train and the edge of reality.

## Neighbour peering from behind the curtains

Do you throw out your garbage every day?

I try not to.
At least sometimes I try not to.
At least sometimes I try to process it into nothingness,
or failing that into something hidden,
something stored only inside me.

The problem is
whenever I do keep it in for any length of time
I eventually throw it out as old garbage,
garbage no longer in its original form
more rotten and stinky
more repulsive to the senses.

I wish, of course, I could recycle it into something useful
- joy or understanding
or
God forbid
even
grace.

I wish I could turn it into a story
or, better still,
a life.

Because I can do none of these things
I avoid the garbage collectors
when they stride down our street
every second Wednesday in the month
purposeful and gloved,
loud, tattooed and sweating,
leaving the empty bin

without thought of position or consequence
somewhere outside my gate.

I feel they mock me.

## The General makes his plan

Three nights ago my left tricep started twitching.
It twitched for nearly an hour
between 9 and 10.

It has done so every night since
same time
same place
- just above the elbow.

It's the part of my arm called the Anconeus muscle.
I know because I Googled it.
I now know everything about the Anconeus muscle
apart from how to stop it twitching
and how to make it start.

For the last 3 nights
my Anconeus has twitched
without my intention, desire or permission.
It has twitched for reasons that remain unknown.
It has twitched despite me.

This evening
my wife is travelling on a plane to Singapore.
She will return in 2 weeks.

Tonight
whilst I sleep
my heart will keep beating.

Tomorrow
the sun will rise.
I will awake
and assume control.

## The academic considers as she runs

Funny things, thoughts.
They change as we do,
or we change as they do,
or perhaps it's a bit of both.
To be honest
I'm not really sure.

I do know I have a certain relationship with my thoughts,
we do clearly relate,
we do influence each other.

It's a relationship that has lasted for as long as I can
remember.

We grew up together,
my thoughts and me,
walking and running and thinking
learning and thinking
looking and thinking
listening and thinking
sometimes too busy thinking to look, listen or learn.

Time for myself
still means time to be alone with my thoughts,
a well-established, ever-expanding room
- a bar with light and shade
murmur and mayhem
owned
yet never quite controlled
by me -
filled with necessary, interesting, unexpected
and sometimes unwelcome
characters.

The loudest relive the past
- my past -
in ways that justify their existence,
imagining my future
according to their need.

Others appear harmless
I fall for their familiarity
and let them build a debt without challenge.

Some sit in the shadows
present
without ever fully drawing my attention.
A few visit only once
never to return.
Sometimes they have such presence,
a promise left unsaid,
I wish I had engaged them more.

There is a space, too, beyond the bar.
Occasionally I sense the entrance and the silence within,
and then my thoughts clamour
objecting to my momentary disregard
calling for my service,
creating the doubts and questions that serve them best.

We have a certain relationship,
my thoughts and me,
and
for all its ups and downs
for all the noise, dark corners and missed opportunities,
it's quite OK.

I think.

## Pensioner admits

I don't know if it's true,
that story I tell about how,
when I was eleven years old,
the gypsy boy chased me on his bike,
pressing hard
a fork gripped between his teeth,
wanting to stab me
for no other reason than I had cycled past.

And how I escaped
by crossing the train line
only seconds before the 3.48 to Nottingham thundered
through.
And how we became friends
or, at least, I turned him into my protector
because he came to our school
- transferred from another –
and I was clever and he wasn't
so I taught him how to trade.

Whenever someone wonders when and why
I chose my life's profession
I cite that story,
seeing only ever the same details in my mind.

You might ask when I first created those pictures,
or settled on those words.
They are, indeed, good questions.

The truth is I don't know when I turned that happening into
a story,
when the ego of my later self massaged my memory,
or even if it is has.

I know only that my past is now a series of stories
that might or might not be true
to a greater or lesser degree;
stories I need to tell
stories that reinforce the mystery
stories that spawn others
some of them yours.

So what do you want to know about me?
What do you want to ask?
I will answer anything as honestly as I can.

Be aware, though, all I have left are stories.
I can't guarantee anything more.

## Par for the course

Thank you, Father for attacking me with your 7-iron.
The one you used
to kill the grey and white cat
when I was just a boy.
The grey and white cat asleep beneath your green and black Westminster,
crippled by the right back wheel as we pulled away,
spine crushed,
head movement exaggerated by the static fur.
One careful swing, head down, gaze fixed, no follow-through needed,
silenced that.

Thank you for waiting in the drive,
stamping and stumbling,
swinging and muttering;
caught in the swirl of loss
anger filling the space
where the-man-I-knew used to live.
Thank you for your rage
- no careful swings this time,
no practice shot,
ruined above the neck but not below.
So, watch out Chris!
One could, indeed, take your head off.

Thank you then,
for holding on just long enough for me to reach you,
to hear you say,
*My head hurts*
once or twice
- or was it three times? -
before the silence came.

Thank you for sharing your life so fully,
for teaching me the most important thing:
how to find the greatest lesson in the greatest pain.
This, I know, was your special gift.

Or, perhaps, as Mother said
I'm just a naïve fool.

## Memories and other clutter

Which to feel most sorry for?

The sock left behind,
a long-time unnoticed loner amongst twins,
or the one gone missing,
lost somehow in the turbulence of cleansing?

I held on to one sock;
not in the drawer with all the others
but above, in the corner,
with the shoelaces
and the fingerless, originally white, shoe-cleaning mitt.

I say *held on*
when, in truth, I pushed to one side
after a brief, casual search for its other half.

I say *held on*
when it would be more honest
to say *left in its spot*
grew used to it just being there.

Our cleaner was careful to return one sock precisely after dusting
- not paid to correct or question she tidied tat with equal care
-
and yet somehow, I don't know when,
it went just like its long-lost partner.

We felt no sense of surprise or loss;
things just shift place
inside or out.

One sock was measured by its other;
an equal part of something
or nothing at all.

Storage alone is never proof of care or need.

## A student graduates

My teachers taught about Creativity
as if it was a subject designed only to be assessed
removed from how they were right then and there
how we were as students
how I was
as me

as if it had nothing to do
with how we dressed
and spent our money
how we believed and thought and acted

as if it had nothing to do
with the mortgage they paid
the role they played
the philosophy they prayed to

as if it was just a transferable skill
a box ticker
a government pleaser

as if it wasn't life.

## Prisoner peering through the bars

The air I need
is always just beyond me
around me
outside.

I inhale and call it Breath
I claim ownership
unaware of the transformation
taking place within.

Sometimes
seeking to relax
I slow my breath
as if the driver of a train easing into a station.

Sometimes
exerting myself
I use breath forcefully
too obviously
disconnected despite the effort.

Other times
my breath creates a rhythm of its own
running away with me
making me shudder to its beat.

Mostly, though, I'm too caught up in things
to notice the intimacy of the in-breath
or the out
- when my breath becomes air again
if, indeed, it ever changed
and some part of me leaves
never to return.

If only we could travel outside
move past our skin for just a second
- even less -
just enough for absolute connection.

If we could be there once
all fear would end.

What would we do?

## Mums before breakfast

The young mother eases her baby's pram
through the impatient crowd,
time on her side
already athlete-fit
she coos and steers
her daughter's face plum-red, wide-eyed,
peering out beneath pink winter wool.

Further back an old man loses ground
shuffling steps
steaming breath
behind his wife's scuffed wheelchair.
She is wrapped in age-old
scrunched down
seeing every crack in the pavement.

## *This*

I don't know how this happened.

Genuinely, I have no idea.

*This* of all things,
how can this possibly be?

I mean, if you ask me
- if you ask anyone -
we'd all say it doesn't make sense given the great churn of possibility
the random turning of thought and skin
the endless shifts of inside and out.

Let's be honest
the odds were stacked against
so high I'm amazed they didn't come tumbling down
and cover everything.

I accept
of course
things have to happen

in a dream
at a concert or the beach
sometimes on a Wednesday

but when the odds are truly stacked against?

That's proof of the pointlessness of planning
or the need to hope,
it's the reason to believe in God
or gamble big into the darkness.

And yet
despite the odds
we met, talked and became
friends.

Incredible, isn't it?

Proof of something.

## Martin learns at night

The house had been demolished.
Now, in the surprisingly small rectangle of earth
amid the sparse patches of grass
human remains litter the footprint of a home

a plastic bottle
several bricks
pages from a free paper
shards of glass, some half-buried, pointing heavenward
as if planted in some unfathomable design,
a used condom
- I think, it is dark I don't investigate too closely –
a single training shoe
an empty cigarette packet

these are the things I notice
all muddied
or in shadow
or a combination of the two
it's hard to tell
as tears blur my vision
and the moon hides its gift beyond the ceiling of cloud.

Who would have thought that this
garden
of all things
could...

Could...

I have to get past me to get to you.

That's the truth
hidden behind the need for right and wrong
for learning facts and proving points
for making a career and establishing a reputation
dividing and classifying
growing the I of isolation
perfectly.

Now I know that I have to get past me to get to you.
Because I am always there
wherever I turn,
the gate keeper
cloaked in intellect and thought
self-interest
and fear,
separate
no matter how close we seem.

I am always there
wherever I turn
filling space with words and thought,
the blinkers of expectation
reflecting ever inwards.

Weakness is my only hope
the challenge to all I have created.
It isn't love, lust or desire that will get me to you
it is submission
reduction
the most holy defeat.

I have to get past me to get to you.

I have to get past me
with a warm smile and a loving arm.

## Explorer

When I clean my teeth
which I do twice every day
I find myself thinking of others.

I think of what they said and what they did
what I believe they thought and what I think they meant
about the clarity of their agenda
compared to the complexity and confusion of my own.

This is not an intentional activity
neither is it a sign of desire or welcome
rather it reflects a borderless land
my mind more public park than protected environment
a space open to all
just wander in and make your mark
don't mind me.

And wander in they do
in ones and twos and sometimes more
not just family or friends
or even acquaintances
but strangers too.

I do my best to create order
to turn this interminable weaving into a well-fitting design
something that explains more than just me or my
circumstance
something that makes thinking or talking or walking
comfortable and secure.

Truth to tell
despite my best efforts
it rarely feels satisfactory.

My internal socialising is, it seems, unstoppable
I am drawn in not only when I clean my teeth
but whenever I have a moment or more alone.

My so-called quiet moments rarely are,
shared instead with the community in my mind.

I am, I guess, in their minds too
making my own noise
leaving my imprint
passing through or lingering.

Perhaps I've been looking for myself in the wrong place?

## innocence turns

our grown-up questions strip us bare
                                                    and wide

public and open

more revealing than mere nakedness
more deliberate than a curtain-glimpse
each aspect peeling back a layer:

topic, framing, words and posture
breath, expression and inflexion
timing, placement and intention

striptease
to insightful eyes and ears

look!
a glimpse of ego
curved inside the frame of expertise

watch!
the opening of the trap
power flashing in the light

listen!
to hesitation catching
soft as fabric
on release

feel!
the need to just belong
bring something out
- a willing trade

roll up!
sit back
enjoy the show:
the exhibitionism of asking
leaving raw the source
pink-fleshed to view

the wrap of curiosity
a long-time lost.

## Years apart

Sometimes we release the question without meaning to.

'Where is nowhere?' I heard myself ask.

'It's heaven,' my grandson said without looking up from his crayoning. 'It's God's home.'

'Perhaps he's right,' I thought later as I walked to the shops. 'Try as I might I am always somewhere. And something's getting in the way.'

## Somewhere

How does the Zen Master
deep within his meditation
know
when to open his eyes?

## Insight

See
artists without choice
galleried
in streets and homes and offices
and all the other well-established places
trapped by design
returning to the same work
endlessly.

The face is their canvas
framed by change - real or imagined -
with lines drawn
the way all artists do,
from the inside out.

Lines on a face

a portrait of journeys
taken
and underway,
stories
complete
or being created.

Lines on a face

offering insights
and reminders

secrets etched into skin
drawing the ebb and flow

a work in progress until the very end
or just before

a life condensed
mapped and moving

*just look*

## Beyond the shoulders

destruction comes first

the mantra of each heartbeat
unheard behind the thud of thought
yet persistent in its great service

destruction

washes clean the screen of vision
strips awareness bare
making bright the space beyond the shoulders

where insight flashes

illuminating lines

## The old man at 102
## talks about saying a word

the deepest pool
one syllable wide
so often there, so easily missed
no attention given
no laying of cloaks
stepping on or over
en route always

unless

control your breath and dive
heart-first
plumb narrow depths
a single word
so dark and dense all senses bow
horizon-free

once lost
inhale
and be surprised
then
drink and drink
through every pore

return
forgetful
vacuum-fresh
then
feeling earth
and all within
let sound come forth
filled and overflowing.

## Mouth to mouth

Words travel on the breath
varied as clouds
changing atmosphere and mood
casting shadow, creating life

breath
rushes excited words
barely formed, tumbling, crashing
scrambling for traction

breath
fires a shout into the atmosphere
softens a whisper beneath the door frame
raises the question
lowers the command

breath
shapes the rhythm of your teaching
shares your sigh
makes your passion gasp

we have lain together curved as one
breathing in perfect union
primal
safe
an island undiscovered by all the rest
and still

words travel on the breath

shared
just like a kiss
just like a bomb

## Prayer for Max

'Max doesn't like pasta.'

He says this, red-cheeked and serious,
talking to the food first
as if it can understand
as if it needs to know, is somehow capable of transformation,
he says this shaking his head solemnly
the way his mother does when she tells him 'No.'

Max doesn't like pasta.
At least at this table.
He has every time before
as far as anyone could tell.
Today something has changed
and it isn't the cooking.

Today
with a frown and a flush
with tomato sauce clumped around his lips
and a fork dropped deliberately into his bowl
Max has marked his difference
made the first shift towards the confusion of identity.

One day he will stop talking to food as if it can hear.
He will stop bringing toys to life
being transfixed by a passing bus
jigging on the spot with uncontrollable excitement.

The door will close gradually on his openness to surprise.
Education and expectation will press him to fill his moments
rather than live them
to greet others politely
laugh with restraint.

Max will be taught how to fit in
squeezed into qualifications
filtered through experience
shaped more by the needs of others
than the food he eats.

For some time now society,
the great conformist snake,
has been sneaking into his life
applying its pressure.

It will become less subtle.

Learning through play, movement and modelling
will be replaced by the race to raise hands into the air
laughter turning quickly into tears and quickly back again
slaughtered in favour of seriousness
he will be taught to fear mistakes
and about the absolute need, above all things, to *know*
encouraged towards an apprenticeship
or a graduate job
- a path shaped by the agendas and rewards of others -
he will be distanced from his birth gift
and
truly blessed
if those close to him
link arms and brace themselves on his behalf against the pressure
standing firm
giving him the time and space he needs to seek his passion
the courage to find his own way.

Today Max doesn't like pasta.

I pray
when he's fifty
he loves his life.

## Martin reflects

I loved once without thinking

briefly

in the mid of night;

now
as I try to express this most glorious oneness
each word acts as a stepping stone
back
to the normal place.

I loved once without thinking

only it wasn't me.

## If God exists

A lover explains:

If God exists
we do not.

Not in the way our parents claimed
hemmed in, despite their love,
by their own experience.

Not in the way our teachers taught us
stitched to a syllabus
direction set to ensure endless repetition of what already is.

Not in the way society presses us
weaving tales of ownership, obligation and limitation
stretching us in its own image.

If God exists
we truly do not.

Not in any way other than this:
both inside and out
intimately connected
nothing more than the smallest thing
nothing less than all there is.

## Watching migrants flee

A wise man wrote
*Society is measured by the strength of its warriors' tears.*

I am blessed

moving inevitably along the circle's upward curve
feeling the circumference drawing together with steady pace
I find myself crying often
and easily.

I cry not because the gap is closing
or for the loss of left behind
I cry for all the reasons the world offers
- the success, failure, pain and hope of others
the stories I choose to believe
because they feel as if the storyteller knew me
the sparrows in the hedgerow claiming ownership -
I cry tears of joy
for the sheer unlikeliness of life.

Tears, I realise, are my wealth
a sign of security
and connection
the greatest reminder I am far removed
from the dried desolation of the dispossessed.

Sometimes I can forgive those who incite my tears of anger
but only, still, when I know them well enough.

## Without borders

There is something else in the wind
something drawn from its endless travels
something circling at its own pace
timeless
beyond number.

We breathe it
in and out
that something else from far-off places
the deserts, seas and mountains
city streets and racing clouds
the different heats of different emotions
the first cries
the last gasps
beliefs we've never held
touching skin
coating lungs
fuelling blood.

There is something else in the wind
something transformed and transforming
a part of it is you
a part of it is me.

## Sawdust

A grain of sawdust
one single speck in the inevitable crowd
framed by the dark colours of the shed
draws my attention in the half-light of the morning.

I don't know why this particular one
I simply watch as the speck
forced into being by an irresistible movement
rises briefly
before the fall begins.

I track it
slowing it's descent in my mind's eye
singling it from the rest

one grain

falling thousands of miles
from where I sit
alone in my study
in the place I start and end each day.

One grain
real and true
drawing me out.

Tonight
perhaps
another place will beckon
another movement so far away it can only be seen
with eyes closed.

## Astronaut

Some believe a God created everything
most of which is Space.

It is the space between the beads that holds them together
the emptiness around the words that gives them shape
the distance between one and the other in which reality
exists.

We say people need space in which to grow
and we have the Universe
which is space enough even for the impossible.

Space is the source of our greatest gifts
those we receive and those we give

it is the maker of relationships
the place beyond the edge
the secret in the depths of silence

space dares us to explore.

In the darkness of a Winter's night
my wife turns on our bed
asleep, she reaches out
pressing the sole of her foot against my calf.
Her toes grip as if holding on to something precious.

She sighs.

I look out through the gap I always leave in the curtains
see a star
briefly
before the clouds cross

- a temporary pretence.

## Rosary

Imagine a business selling only the very best of reminders
personal to all.

Imagine the demand
the queues
the certainty of requirement;
the difficulty in meeting need would be the challenge
each bead a different weight and shape and colour
each connection so different from another.

Easier, then, to sell other gifts
many lost in re-creation
at best disfigured when transferred.

We can, it seems, share only so much before
all else disappears below the surface.

You are it
my rosary
reminder of what matters most
touchpoint in busy times
prayer
purpose
and hope
always.

You are it
my defence against the worst of me
my belief in something more.

## The healer wishes

I wish I could open my case
take silence out
and breathe it gently
unnoticed
into the minds of others

breathing through eyes and ears
nostrils too
riding the in-breath
sneaking silence
as the conscious rattles

I wish silence was mine enough to share
that I could be its willing servant
the carrier from shore to shore
grateful for the opportunity
to play my part

only

I cannot bear silence for any length of time against the
current
not when the horizon threatens
when noise rolls in and crashes
when options dance
or success squeezes.

I have
on occasion
stumbled into silence
felt it seeping from the outside in
and the inside out
heard the words that grow there, perfect in their form,

drawing all together
whilst the rest of me gathered
sure of its loud return
urgent to pour back into the fleeting space.

Of all things I believe this:

there is silence
the most natural home
deep within us
too often crushed beneath the noise we create
and the need for more
and
        more
and
        then
with waves crashing
we isolate the words of others
colour them with our own dark dangers
hold them to account
and fuel the storm we call
normality.

Truly, I would be the carrier of Silence
grateful for the opportunity
to share its secret
and breathe it to your own
to meet you there
to see your beauty
and know your truth

in silence.

## Algebra

If I knew you more
I would surely know you less;
the passion of not-knowing
the great curiosity of love
the hunger of longing
all choked by the ever-tightening noose of certainty
- that most caustic divide.

If I knew you more
I would surely know you less;
blinded to the surprise of you by the inevitability of understanding
separated from doubt and joy and hope
- the life blood of the devotee -
by the slowly suffocating blanket-warmth of expertise.

When young
I sought knowledge the way a new-born seeks the breast.
I was drawn only towards that which, captured and contained,
encouraged more
fed my need to build;
knowledge was my security and my source of growth
the way I defined and hid and tricked myself
and others too.

You brought the power of mystery
the always-present and the disappearance
the sweet scent
the moist kiss
the oh-so-close unknown.

You taught something else entirely
something beyond measurement or boundary
balanced exquisitely on the very beginning
more than the greatest answer
more, even, than any sense of me:

Knowing + not knowing = love and faith.

The perfect equation.

## Who?

*A question of love*

I sleep so well with you beside me
because I know you better than anyone else on earth.
This is my comfort through life's changes.

It seems to me
- and there's the risk -
that to know someone so well
and be known in return
is one of the great treasures we all seek,
a need crossing boundary and border
the place where lost and found and lost again
spiral
ever
inward
until the point of difference is so diminished
and so disguised
it seems to disappear.

And yet
I understand you in the only way I know how
from the living place behind my eyes,
eyes with their own blind spot
relying on their significant other to help me navigate my way.

Perhaps we have worked together in silent agreement
to construct this life within a narrow row of understanding,
a street lined with buildings that function as walls
keeping us in whenever we are together
adding their shadows to our own
limiting our vision
and oh, so rich for all that.

Perhaps our love-trained eyes
see each other so well within the confines of all we have created
we miss the movement in the shadow

the otherness beyond the knowing.

This morning I sat waiting for your return
- one simple word, syllables ocean-deep, teeming with time apart, comfortable within its basic construct -
whilst I, for all my magnificent design,
struggled to contain anticipation
and the swirling, swelling pride of a well-planned surprise.

I knew you wouldn't see me
ensconced in the burgundy armchair
leather-worn, experienced as an old man lined by every trick and change
tucked away in the corner of the grand hotel reception, sitting there
counting down the minutes
watching the street through large glass doors
watching the men with close-cropped hair and attentive eyes
uniformed in their old-fashioned coats
greeting arrivals with at least half-a-smile
as if this was fair exchange for what they used to do.

I knew you wouldn't see me there
- just one more stop on your journey home -
no expectation now of recognition or reunion.

Only you, forever the great teacher,
forged a lesson as you always do,
the present from your travels
inescapable as the new day

and mine only, a broadening of that narrow row,
too much between-us for even men in coats to recognise.

It began before you left the taxi
something different in your profile
and your gesture
clear despite the half-shadow
clearer still as you stepped out
comfortable with the crammed cases tracking at your heel
like well-trained dogs.

I couldn't have known
- was not prepared for -
what the chair must have witnessed so many times with so many others
just one of its well-kept secrets:

this was you alone

you
I had never seen before

you
without me

finding your way
clear-eyed despite the travel
you
in your own shining space

you
the protector of my sleep.

Easy then
as I watched

you
walking without requirement
alone
freed from the need to show your love for anyone but
yourself
easy then
to be thankful for the new question
beacon-bright
filled with wonder:

Who are you
my love
when I'm not there?

Who?

## Our garden

### (i)

For one who grew up in the countryside
who, as a boy, worked the Manor grounds
and for a penny would lay the scent
running joyously before the hounds and men on horseback
whippet-lean
more heart than head
who grew to work for thirty years or more outside
sometimes sleeping in the field
using earth and sky as home,
for a man who spent nearly half his span like this
he didn't care too much for gardening.

Not that he ever disregarded it
he was too proud to leave anything untended.
Rather he kept things simple
no complex planting
no borders requiring explanation
no demanding designs,
choosing instead the bare, easy minimum:

a squared lawn
lined on three sides by roses not-quite evenly spaced
a simple path with no clear edge
a corner shed, secure but drab as a mongrel's sodden fur,
a grey slab patio
hosed down whenever it was demanded of him.

Our garden.
Not so different from all the rest
not as bright and shiny as those rare few
but not the worst

- he made sure of that -
not as bad as no17 where one fence panel always needed replacing
and 23 where even the front showed signs of couldn't-care-less.

I never asked him if he was secretly grateful for 17 and 23
or what purpose he thought the garden served
or if it ever reminded him of when he could run forever
or if it ever stirred a Union man's anger that money and land always went together
or if he ever expected to end with this particular space.

I had no questions about our garden
beyond the occasional 'Must I really?'
I had no questions about our garden just as I had no questions about
our kitchen or our lounge, or that print of the talking dogs.

I had no questions about how my parent's life
– the frame of mine -
had reached this point
if this had always been their plan
if this was *it*
and if so, why?

Our garden stayed that way forever
or so it seemed.
If I'd thought at all
I would have thought
this garden, just like Thatcher, isn't for turning.
Only I was wrong, just like she was wrong
and it had nothing to do with the seasons

no planetary change caused this turn
nothing to do with our so-called Earth spinning through the heavens

and certainly
nothing
to do
with a change of heart
a sudden desire to create
something new

outshine the neighbours.

Instead
a buildup and a burst
an everyday crash and collapse
pathways burning
curling inward
in the heat.

It took some weeks
that slow reveal
late winter weeks
the garden showing no signs of life.

When he came home
the routes to mind and mouth
were broken;
we shared
unspeakable detours to previously unknown places.

His body, of course, fought back
ferociously so
no hounds and horses now

but still more heart than head
more heart than head

still needing to move.

**(ii)**

The spade, brown-handled, rusting, not cleaned since the last time
looked bigger against him than before
as if it had grown in hibernation and knew that he had shrunk
as if it was throwing down a challenge
as out of the shed he came
his grim determination fixed on the lawn
not yet ready to be cut
and never again to be so.

We didn't know and didn't ask
not then
not ever
- well, not of him.

Instead we all agreed:
he's safe in his own garden.

Our garden.

We can keep an eye on him here.
At least he can't wander
or make a nuisance of himself.

Is that really what we said?
*Can't make a nuisance?*

He needed both hands now
the spade
heavy
carried like a rifle from hip to shoulder;
not a deliberate gesture on his part
no making a point
more bare than that, more stripped right down,
mask-less now and until the end
moving forward
one foot dragging slightly
head jutting, threatening always to overbalance,
moving because that is, of all things, the most basic sign,
moving with enough skin
just
to contain
those blue-grey veins
and shining knuckles
and beating heart
enough skin just to keep him in,
the thinnest of prison walls
- impenetrable none the less -
a most solitary confinement
no visitor can enter here
no one escapes.

Love hurts one-way.

He stamped down hard
anger his heart's engine
forcing metal into earth
one, two, three, four initial cuts
isolating one misshaped piece from all the rest
then back to the beginning:

1. Spade in and under
2. Scoop green-topped soil
3. Balance briefly on the spade, snorting, staring,
4. Return, upended, into the waiting grave
5. Begin again.

No looking back
just stamp and cut time after time
isolate, remove, return inside-out
just do this thing
stamp-cut-lift-balance-tip
just take the lawn and turn it upside down
and turn it into something else
just kill the grass and show the soil
dare roots to grow in public view
just dig and turn 'till there's nothing left

there's nothing left.

Did we say that?

**(iii)**

It took a day
for him to turn our lawn inside out.
He never tried to turn it back again.
He tried instead to talk to us

only the lawn hadn't freed him
and the lawn didn't help us gain entry
the soil just lay there, secure but drab as a mongrel's sodden fur,
and he tried to kill himself
twice

and people saved him
twice.

And then, eventually, there was no saving.

The ending came
natural as the soil
although it felt less drab.

**(iv)**

It's not our garden anymore.
It doesn't look the same.
The borders are more vibrant
the shed is new
the path well-edged
the patio re-paved.
The lawn is now a luscious green.

There's much beneath it.

***********

**conversations**
**about**

**the**

**dot**

**at the**

**centre**

**of the circle**

**circle:**

a curved line that is the same distance from the centre all the
way around
and connects at the point where it began.

*'If your mind asks,*
*"How can I understand the Almighty?"*
*Tell it simply and firmly that it cannot.*
*Say all it needs to know is that*
*the Almighty*
*is the always present, all-encompassing Being of the Universe.*
*Tell it then to ignore questions that are sent to trick it.'*

*If your mind asks,*
*"What is Death?"*
*Tell it*
*"Death is the end of Consciousness*
*as Consciousness understands itself.*
*So forget it!"*

*'If your mind asks,*
*"What is Life?"*
*Tell it*
*"Life is the dot at the centre of the circle.*
*So strip all else away!"*

Epiah Khan

## Poison

It was 2am in a hotel bar in Southeast Asia. The lesson had started a couple of hours earlier. My teacher was in full flow, shrinking my world down into the space between us, clogging my breathing and thinking.

'Do you remember,' my teacher asked, 'your question from a year ago, when we first came here?'

'Yes.' I nodded, trying to disguise my uncertainty. That night I had asked several questions before he had silenced me in his usual manner.

My teacher's eyes glittered. 'What was it?'

My mind raced. My teacher lit a cigarette whilst I sought to avoid commitment.

There was no escape. The pressure forced words out. They scrambled for traction like a man's feet on a steep shale hillside.

'It was a...a question about names,' I said.

He stared at me; blew smoke out of his nose. I couldn't help but glance at the scars on his forearms. He waited. Silence had been his ally for as long as I had known him. I felt obliged to say more.

'I asked you to tell me the name of the martial art you study.'

'And?'

'And you leant forwards and glared at me and asked if I really thought that names mattered. And I realised it was a stupid question and said that of course names don't matter; it's what we do that matters. And you lit a cigarette and changed the subject.'

My teacher took a crumpled piece of paper from out of his pocket and handed it to me. 'Read this,' he said.

I did. It was a name, the answer to my question of a year ago.

'Of course names matter!' He slapped my shoulder hard. 'Now, go and buy yourself a drink.'

I returned to see a small container filled with a dark yellow liquid on the table in front of my chair.

'It's poison,' my teacher said. 'It shouldn't kill you. Drink it.'

I stared into his glittering eyes, then down at the liquid, then back into his eyes.

There was no escape. The pressure forced words out. They scrambled for traction...

In hindsight I am sure those around us were living their lives too.

## A poem wounds

The water's edge, where lines blur, beckons like a gentle
hand
or crashes down a brazen dare
no matter which the choice is yours
some cautious steps or a rush and dive
into a place so close
so strange
salt-flavoured swirl
with pull and drag

and rocks beneath the surface bite

and sometimes through the jagged tear comes laughter
and sometimes comes a scream
and sometimes comes a still, deep knowing

and later
on dry land again
letting distance in
you name it.

The question was accepted with only the slightest of shifts,
a stone breaking the surface with barely a splash
enveloped in a heartbeat
the speed of its descent determined by its form and the current
ending somewhere unseen
displacing a fragile layer
or settling atop something more secure
- impossible to tell from the shoreline.

A moment of silence
stillness
a search flickering over eyes and skin
diving down
and then
selection made
the answer rising from the depths.

'Repetition,' the old man at 102 said, 'you can never get enough of it.' He paused briefly. 'Repetition,' he said again, 'is also a falsehood wrapped in the falsehood of time mapped in the falsehood of memory used as the building block of stories. Yet repetition is essential for testing and teaching, development, distraction and, most important of all, fishing.'

'Fishing?'

'Requires distance,' the old man at 102 nodded, 'and the willingness to seem stupidly forgetful. It also requires curiosity and connection, great timing and selection, sequencing and care.'

'And what do you fish for?'

'Insight.'

'And how do you fish?'

'You disappear, cast out something appropriate and be receptive.'

'And then?'

The old man at 102 shrugged. 'Who knows?'

'Why do you say repetition is a falsehood?'

'The old man at 102 tapped his forefinger four times against his forehead. 'Because repetition, repetition, repetition, repetition, only exists in the human mind. You'll realise that's true if you tell yourself often enough.'

'Are you being serious?'

The question was accepted with only the slightest of shifts,
a stone breaking the surface with barely a splash
enveloped in a heartbeat
the speed of its descent determined by its form and the current
ending somewhere unseen
displacing a fragile layer
or settling atop something more secure
- impossible to tell from the shoreline.

A moment of silence
stillness
a search flickering over eyes and skin
diving down
and then
selection made
the answer rising from the depths.

The room is filled with an array of objects
so much attraction for busy eyes:

lights and lamps
paintings and photos
tables nested
flowers arranged and watered
scratches, scuffs, creases, tears
the scars of living
framed by colour and curtain.

Two chairs dominate
the finest leather
malt whisky shades
lined by age and use

chairs for sitting, watching, reading, sleeping,
losing socks and coins, spilling wine and food,
climbing if you are small enough

chairs for holding time, soothing minds,
easing back

chairs that demand attention.

The space between them comes from the stars
the first of all mothers
both river-flow and cradle
to our man-made.

The room is filled with an array of objects
two chairs dominate
the universe passing through unnoticed.

The gift
you gave
was
wrapped
in many layers

the
first

such bright attraction
- mystery balanced boldly on the edge of promise -
standing out from all around
demanding, daring, drawing me in
rapid eyes and hands desperate for reveal

the
second

so delicate at first touch
took more time to open
needing the light and warmth
and occasional rain
of season change
the space and fuel for roots to grow
the courage to continue

the
third

complex in nature
took longer still
some parts more fearful than others
glued tight and clinging
releasing slowly over time
soothed by the warmth of my searching

my desire to know what your gift could be
the reason why so many layers were needed

and then
I realised

it was your life.

It began the morning the old man first thought of sleep as a little death.

The thought itself wasn't a consequence of anything he was aware of. It was consequential, however. It did spark the question,

*How many little deaths are there?*

He began looking and counting.

*Two.*
The flower shrivelling naked before the cold.

*Three*
A qualification gained.

*Four*
A question blocked by fear.

*Five*
The beginning of a journey.

*Six*
Learning language.

*Seven*
The first intimacy.

*Eight*
Giving birth.

*Nine*
The first grandchild.

He stopped looking and counting when he reached 102.

He knew by then he was loved.

She wrote:

I longed to drink cocktails sat at the bar
he said we'd sit by the fire and sip wine.
He wanted to make me a mother
I wanted to make us both rhyme.

We'd met at a place with a bar and a beach
the moon was full, he called it a sign.
We made love on the sand with the stars shining down
I heard the sound of the waves and they rhymed.

The plans in my head and the dreams in my mind
and the love and the lust all combined.
He felt like the man who could be all the things
I needed to make my life rhyme.

We bought the great house with a bath made for two
I knew his body just as I knew mine.
We touched and we washed and we played and we kissed
turning movement, I thought, into rhyme.

I supported his work, enjoyed plotting his rise
cheered from the side as he climbed;
his title, his pay, his clothes and his car came together
I could hear how they rhymed.

The children were great, changing schedules and strength
my love growing fierce as I watched their eyes shine.
He did what he could with the demands of his day
I always soothed them to sleep with a rhyme.

And I'd be up in the night when they called out for more
feeding and soothing and acting a mime
far more than a role or a sense of the moon
feeling love and a loss in a rhyme.

So when I longed to drink cocktails and sit at the bar
and he said we'd sit by the fire and sip wine
I felt like a part so essential to me
had been lost and left far behind.

'You know what I need,' I said, close to the edge.
'I need to make us both rhyme.'
'Just trust me. I promise we will,' he replied.
'It's only a matter of time.'

I let her run her story over me.

I let her use my senses and skin as a training ground
turning words and sentences and sequencing, gestures and expressions
into well-rehearsed plays
- both offensive and defensive -
incorporating feints and distractions
associations intended to mislead and misdirect
memories chosen to act as proof-points.

I let her run and refine her story across my mind
repeating reasons to be right
developing confidence
filling foundations
building what would later be called truth
needing to win, however that's defined
needing to be safe, whatever that means.

And through it all she was most welcome
there was no deliberate deceit on her part
and there comes a time when,
beyond the dearest,
all that is left is being either teacher or training ground.

Once, perhaps, I would have closed the gates and put up the sign
now I have no need to be so self-supporting
I've lived enough
lost the desire to climb the moral heights
where the air's too thin
and the view too clouded to encourage anything other than
*I made it to the top.*

So I let her in
and I let her stay for as long as she needed
and whilst she twisted and turned
whilst she instinctively created her protection and springboard
unaware of quite what was happening
I remembered how many times I had done the same in my life.

We all need somewhere to practise.

He read the first book first
and the second book second.
He said the first was great
and the second he didn't hate.

She read the second book first
and the first book second.
She said the second blew her mind away
and the first, for all its charm, was just OK.

Thank God I met you on a Monday.

It's just a small tree
between two houses
and the sky beyond

it's there most obviously
when we sit
together
at night
sipping wine
holding feet and touching fingers
playing hide and seek in leather chairs
watching recorded programmes

stopping everything
to read the latest story
or view the latest clip
of grandchildren growing

sitting together

releasing gratitude and disbelief
when the first leaves appear
as the red sky holds
at Autumn's gold
or Winter's dark reveal.

It's just a small tree
in a small garden
between two houses
and the sky beyond

we watch the seasons passing through
clinging and releasing

I watch my wife
staring at the tree

clinging and releasing.

I asked:

‘Who are you my love when I’m not there?

Who?’

You smiled
took my hands in yours
kissed me gently
and whispered in my ear

buildings disappeared.

The words ran through me
scooshing
overwhelming foreground

I could have called them a poem
if I had managed their containment
and organised their release
only they were there and gone
within and without
so fast

- an unstoppable flow
a desperate mouse
a charging lion -

my belated attempts to latch onto something
missing
            missing
                        missing.

Other things also treat me as route way:
food
drink
the edge of memories
moments of clarity
my fifties

- whoosh! -

by then I always had a pen at the ready
and still I was too late.

Shame.

My fifties could have been a poem too.

The building reaches higher than all the rest
part workplace
part tourist-draw
pulling crowds inwards and up
inviting wonderment and pride
a design shout-out impossible to ignore
- above all things, *this*

unless the helicopter passing by at eye-level
or the plane higher still
spark the sometime thought
of other lives precious as our own
and the casual trio
Who? Where? Why?
distract briefly

or the sun
the nearest great-distant
reflects on metal, making eyes squint,
before pulling vision to the heavens
and the ever-expanding too-big-to-be-seen

or a child cries
and adult voices offer reassurance
tinged with concern of different types
as eyes glance
all unnoticed by the couple sitting on the false-grass
sipping champagne
drinking promises

or the photos I take
of you
leaning against the glass
face glowing
fear conquered

making sure I capture too
the snakey river and historic roofs

and all the while
lifts run silent up and down
queues form
leavers exit by different routes

every thing
is
secondary

I am not, the wind whispered, the wind bellowed
I am not, the sparrow chirped building in the hedgerow
I am not, the river gushed smoothing rock
I am not, the sea confirmed with all its faces
I am not, the air assured filling his lungs
I am not, the tree promised spreading unseen beneath his feet
I am not, the mountain clamoured whitening in the sky
I am not, the sun glared burning his skin
I am not, the moon sighed disappearing behind a cloud
I am not, the new-born cried, the new-born cried
I am not, the corpse insisted demanding to be kissed
I am not, the clock chimed encouraging him to count

and so he turned his attention to Silence
listening
as he fell into the layered space

he felt it smile
- he believed.

'I'm going to teach the same lesson for the fourth time this week,'
the so-called teacher said.

And the School of Life refused him entry
too busy being Summer easing into Autumn
as never before.

The question was accepted with only the slightest of shifts;
a stone breaking the surface with barely a splash
enveloped in a heartbeat
the speed of its descent determined by its form and the current,
ending somewhere unseen
displacing a fragile layer
or settling atop something more secure
- impossible to tell from the shoreline.

A moment of silence
stillness
a search flickering over eyes and skin
diving down
and then
selection made
the answer rising from the depths.

'Repetition,' the old man at 102 said, 'you can never get enough of it.' He paused briefly. 'Repetition,' he said again, 'is also a falsehood wrapped in the falsehood of time mapped in the falsehood of memory used as the building block of stories. Yet repetition is essential for testing and teaching, development, distraction and most important of all fishing.'

'Fishing?'

'Requires distance,' the old man at 102 nodded, 'and the willingness to seem stupidly forgetful. It also requires curiosity and connection, great timing and selection, sequencing and care.'

'And what do you fish for?'

'Insight.'

'And how do you fish?'

'You disappear, cast out something appropriate and be receptive.'

'And then?'

The old man at 102 shrugged. 'Who knows?'

'Why do you say repetition is a falsehood?'

The old man at 102 tapped his forefinger four times against his forehead, 'Because repetition, repetition, repetition, repetition only exists in the human mind. You'll realise that's true if you tell yourself often enough.'

'Are you being serious?'

The question was accepted with only the slightest of shifts;
a stone breaking the surface with barely a splash
enveloped in a heartbeat
the speed of its descent determined by its form and the current
ending somewhere unseen
displacing a fragile layer
or settling atop something more secure
- impossible to tell from the shoreline.

A moment of silence
stillness
a search flickering over eyes and skin
diving down
and then
selection made
the answer rising from the depths.

The prison of *I*
with its polluted soot-black walls
and constant chatter
deafens inmates.

Martin escaped once.

In the first seconds
he heard
sparrows in the hedgerow
a pigeon taking flight
two men talking
a car gaining speed
a bus squeaking and groaning
a mother whispering to her baby

he heard
his neighbour's dog straining on the leash
footsteps in the drive
the letterbox opening
the pause before the post landed
the scuff and thud as it hit

he heard
the clock in the hallway
wind whistling through ill-fitting windows
and, finally, a heartbeat.

He heard them all
nameless but one
cradled in silence.

He was recaptured soon after.

I reached what I call
a *Decision.*
Then I waited
letting clouds form and
scurry towards it.

I let the clouds darken,
let them gather and weigh down.

I waited
unmoving
until the storm burst
overwhelming the banks of
what I call *Intention.*

I stood on high ground
watching all being swept away
- *washed away* as I called it
because that sounds more hygienic.

I stood on high ground
sheltering beneath
what I recognise as *reason*
and thought
*Back to the drawing board.*

I had what I regarded as
an *Unusual thought*
and handcuffed it promptly to some well-known others;
a cross-cultural chain gang
working the same ground they had yesterday,
filling their most recent excavations,
creating new ones ready for the sunrise.

I developed what I know
to be a *Belief.*
It wasn't a conscious thing
it just snuck up on me
and
all of a sudden
there it was
more obvious than my brain,
more obvious even
than the planet beneath my feet.

I accepted the belief without question,
a thickening of the mask
around my eyes and ears.

I made a stupid *Promise*
because drink drenches consequence
and I chose to keep it
because some principles
- like a handshake -
are more important than
context, condition or content.

I guess, when you add it all together,
I'm not to be trusted.

Still, maybe tomorrow.

His secret:

I prayed to feel an angel's touch
I wanted yours but not so much
yet the devil in you drew me to your fire

the flames reached out
they lapped and burned
my heart withdrew, my senses turned
my soul-less skin was charred upon your pyre

so here we are
this sacred place
it's every step of every race
we go nowhere, the world is lost and burning

we cannot hear
Life's silent sound
we cannot see
the space around
our tongues entwine, the damp bed fuels our yearning

and lies come forth
they enter deep
they score the darkness of our sleep
our skin is changed, its taste transformed forever

and my stomach churns within me
at that night not left behind
and my stomach sends me retching
to the darkest corners of my mind
as my memory fires the time I promised *Never*

I prayed to feel an angel's touch
I paid the price, there is non-such

we soil all colour
with the darkness of our shadows.

I had a great night at the Elton John concert.

She had queued all night to get the tickets.
I didn't know; she didn't tell me until later.

Elton John was amazing.

The night was great.

I can't remember her name.

He confessed:

I could ease my way in to this
only we don't have time to waste
so here it is:

I keep doing the same things
over and over
and some of them are very good for me
and the people I care about
and some of them are bad,
really bad.

I want to keep writing about the bad things
because habit longs to be fed,
because we get used to the devils we know
and forget we should only have angels.

It's the devils that want me to keep writing.

So I'll shut up.

Now

just like -

Damn!

That hurts!

The fish in the bucket overnight
the fish I chased for over an hour
and caught
                and placed in the bucket overnight
the fish that died in the bucket
the fish I killed
                needlessly.

You haven't been gone for long
and already it's killing
but if I make time rhyme
will it put gloss on my loss
and detract from the fact
that I'm broken?

My heart's falling apart
my chest heaving - you took with you my breathing

- and Oxford Street
is too fucking busy!

It's all getting in through the gaps around my eyes and the skin on my ears
and the planet's spinning too fast for my feet
and the forward-looking waves are flooding the banks of my nostrils
stretching my broken nose
and the pavement pulls stronger than any current
and I'm going to be washed up at the foot of that glass-fronted building
where two types of grey meet
and I'm not dressed for it
and those who are will definitely look
and normally I could
but today I don't think I can
convince them that I'm not competition
and I'm not Rambo either
so I might not get back up again
because space shouldn't be this dense
and silence shouldn't be this loud
and that measure of protection I took for granted
has been dragged away by the dark stuff
and I didn't really mean it

- honestly, I didn't really mean it
or, at least, I didn't know what it meant –
when I said

*I want to be like that*
*and live my life like that*

and no one could have stopped me anyway
because I had my own forward-looking wave
and we all choose our own pain
and the dark stuff left laughing
knowing I would be run through by all of

*this*

so where is the cave when you most need one?
and why is the middle of this path so crowded?
and why does resurrection demand so many painful deaths
and why is there no guarantee?
and why is that dog wrapped in a blanket on such a hot day?
and why isn't it looking up?
and why am I the only one sweating?
tumbling in the tide
looking for a place where there's absolutely nothing
only that place doesn't exist
and if it does I can't find it
so there's nowhere to go
and nothing to hold on to
and as my hand reaches out
it's knocked back by the mass
in their summer colours
and if I could I'd grab their design and
press it against the torn, raggedy hole where the dark stuff left
and perhaps that's all I ever was

and perhaps I should have chosen my wardrobe with more care
and why am I the only one sweating?
and my hand reaches out again
because it doesn't know any better
and because it doesn't want to go anywhere near the wound
and this time it's rewarded
somehow, for some reason,
because an angel light appears
and chooses me

and my feet moved towards it
and my mouth spoke
- I know because I heard it -
and a door closed
and suddenly I could press back without falling
and move without spinning
and suddenly I was clutching the lie of distance shamelessly
and although I doubted if I'd ever be able to drool again
it was at least *something*

and that was the first time
according to the only record I can access

and I want to stop thinking about it now.

I've got a conference call to make.

I'm drowning in your voice
thank God
I'm breathing underwater
although the current's turning bloody
as my planet's being slaughtered
by the choices men are making

I'm drowning in your voice
in love
with all the pain I've chosen
and I feel the great wave coming
from where the land's no longer frozen

drowning in your voice
breathing underwater
levels rising, banks are bursting,
giving birth now to Greed's daughter
as the scorched earth lines the future.

Listen to your teachers, son
that's what my parents taught
but there were never any lessons
in how teachers should be sought

I was sent to those who said they knew
the things all teachers should
but they reinforced what I couldn't do
and less those things I could

I didn't drown in any voice
- there was one I swam towards
but I was dragged back to dry land again
because, because, because
imagination isn't real for most
at best, they say, it's harmless fun

but when people can't imagine
they can't see the things they've done

so tomorrow is a shock
a place they visit, never build
yet time and space are all we have
and we make sure they're always filled

and there are needs that must be fed
and there are lies that must be told
so many stories being said
opinions, wrapped, and being sold

so whose voice do I give credence to
and who do I let in?
The voice that drowns is all around
and now it is within:

it's the whisper of the faintest breeze
the rising colour in the heat
the plastic in the oceans
the tightening ground beneath our feet

it's the sound of trees collapsing
and the species that we fail
the silence in the forest
the choking of the whale

it's the changing of the seasons
the scared chirping of the bird
it's the orchestra of Nature
praying to be heard.

I'm drowning in your voice
thank God

I'm breathing underwater
although the current's turning bloody
as my planet's being slaughtered
by the choices men are making

I'm drowning in your voice
my guide
we are dying

hear

together.

The bed
covered in white
first in a row of three

solid
silent
judgement-free

an experienced frame
an indifferent holding
attention drawn to contents
and covers.

'Wake up and stop being so silly!'
She prods the left shoulder
it moves upwards
and in
the eyes glued tight
the mouth-slit boulder-solid.

'Even if you don't wake up
I need you to come home!
I can't live in that house alone!
Listen to me!'

She pushes
punches
- something like -
a mix of fear and anger
and maybe love
who knows what lines a hand?

The body judders
emotion-free
waxen
soon to colour.

'It's OK. You can go now,'
he whispers from the other side.
'Everything is taken care of
so whenever you are ready.'
He squeezes the right hand gently
chest pounding

the bed
a disinfected place
hidden in plain sight.

Once, hoping to create something new,
I told him that I loved him.
He was seventy then.
He stared straight ahead
looking through the windscreen
into the dark November night.
He said the feeling was mutual.
We shook hands as we always did.
I was careful to match his grip as I always did.
We never spoke of it again.

Jean is a grandmother now
despite her prayers.

She adores the baby of course – impossible not to.
She wishes things were different for her daughter
wishes the baby was a boy.

On her way to work
Jean walks passed the charity shop
that had once been a newsagent
that had once been a stationers.

She can only hope they will give her
a few more hours at the petrol station.

Skippy the dog,
part-hound
part-terrier
named after a
fictional kangaroo,
found
Excalibur
in the scrub
at the edge of
the wood.
He raised it with ease
in his drool-flecked
gentle mouth
and brought it back
with ear-flapping urgency,
dropping it at my feet
unaware of his sudden,
undeniable and unexpected
royal claim.

I wiped the sword dry
in the long grass
and took it home
practising cuts as
we walked
Skippy jumping occasionally
for the blade
realising belatedly
perhaps
he had already
surrendered
his throne.

Excalibur
held the magic
of
infinite possibility;
in the following days
I fought and won
a hundred years war,
slayed so many dragons
they were forever driven
from my
imagination,
ruled a mighty kingdom
from a golden castle,
defeated evil at every turn
and made my best friend
a knight.

Then,
inspired by
John Wayne in a
Green Beret
and my friend's new
plastic luger,
Excalibur
transformed
into a
World War 2
sub-machine gun.

The conflict between
us
raged the length of
our street and beyond:
parts of an
allotment

damaged
as bombs
were thrown;
the peace of
the nearby park
shattered,
pensioners' quiet,
reflective time
the inevitable
collateral damage
as I became an expert
at making
the
loudest-ever
sub-machine gun sounds
and taking
numerous bullet wounds
to the chest
without
slowing down
even for a second.

When
the plastic luger
broke
and
a
sulking surrender
was accepted
the sub-machine gun
turned overnight
into
the best
snooker cue
of all time;

every visit
to
the table
guaranteeing
breaks of
147
and a
new world title.

Occasionally,
waking in the
middle of the night,
looking up at
the stars,
the cue
became
a wand,
enabling
moonlit spells
and journeys
to other planets
(returning always
to its sporting form
in time for a
game or two
before breakfast).

Eventually,
of course,
Skippy reclaimed
his stick
as every dog must;
chewing it
unnoticed
into soft, slavvery bits,

leaving them
without a
backward glance
when my father called
and
shook his lead.

Two days later
my friend
found a
stick
of his own;
against its unlimited power
my toys could not
compete.
A new King reigned.

It will be a long time before we are children again.

There's a perfect grief to be found in every losing
There's a perfect grief that spawns every success
There's a perfect grief there for our choosing
It's the perfect grief that creates more from the less.

It can be a moment or a lifetime in the making
It can be feared or the most complete surprise
It can spawn the belief love is just there for the taking
It can make happy ever after seem the best of lies.

Yet the perfect grief holds more than pain and sorrow
Its colours more complex than the scream of *Why?*
It gives strength and hope and brightness to tomorrow
It offers warmth to every passing by.

The perfect grief shapes the best of all our living
The perfect hand at home inside the perfect glove
The perfect grief is Nature's most precious giving
The perfect grief grows from, and then returns, to love.

When the wave
so many miles old
reaches shore

it transforms
as it greets

we play
in the foam of this transformation

we dip our toes
run towards or away from
dive headlong
let it dry, salt-baked, on our skin
wash it away

turn our attention elsewhere.

When the wave
so many miles old
reaches our shore
the mystery of continuation is brought before us

mostly
we call it *holiday*.

The shallows offer the brightest colours
a vibrant mix amid the coral
a source of marvel and wonder
a different world within walking distance
through warm water.

He played there often as a child.
Encouraged by family watching from the shore he
splashed and laughed
tried to catch the darting fish
shared his experiences loudly and often.

It was years later before the first thought of going further
before the darkening of the water beyond the bay
unlocked something close enough to curiosity
for him to feel in control.

He was not prepared for the sudden cold
and the current's drag
the undulating wall of swell,
the isolation.

His breathing quickened
body pimpling pathetically
feet scrambling, treading water, going nowhere.
He forced himself to swim ten more strokes towards the
horizon
and then turned back
racing
using the waves' rush
ignoring the bright colours
feet desperate for the feel of solid ground

That was the first time.
The second was made easier by the memory.

The third warranted only the merest forethought.
The next offered neither purpose nor challenge.

The options reared and swirled like currents clashing:
he had to forget or go deeper still
surrender to the security of what his senses knew
or swim further from the community of the land.

He couldn't sleep for days
and when he finally did, exhausted,
the darkness as his eyes collapsed became
the darkness of the ocean.

He woke fearful and freed.
He couldn't know how far out was far enough,
so he swam until he could see neither coastline nor horizon
until his heart was beating with nameless emotion.

When he could bear that no longer
he stopped his stroke
took one deep breath of salted air
and dived.

The sea seemed oblivious to his descent,
neither welcoming nor resistant,
caring nor confrontational.

He left the light behind with frightening ease.

Pressure came with the darkness
squeezing chest and mind in equal measure
threatening to wrap him
in the deadweight of uncontrollable thought.

He retreated instantly,
desperate for the surface as he had once been for the shore
desperate for the sight of grey cloud
for the sound of a passing sea bird scouring for food.

That night some part of his mind resisted the usual comfort of his bed
fighting instead to keep his eyes open
kicking awake whenever tugged by the deeper recesses of sleep
clinging ferociously to the crumbling cliff-edge of familiarity.

He challenged it
by swimming and diving the next day and the next
the depths becoming an inescapable source of insight and discomfort
his ability to manage his breath enabling him to go ever deeper.

His eyes learnt to adjust
his body became accustomed to the pressure of stillness
to the weight between the in-breath and the out.
The sea squeezed light and life
into different levels of awareness and being.

He was attacked by shadows
some faster than the fastest fish
some heavier than a sunken ship
others, barbed, clung long after the dive had ended
they hurt him often before he recognised them as himself.

Once accustomed to the pain
he began to see movement and colour and change
where he had first been blind
he began to feel at home in the loss of security
and in his own limitation
his feet surrendered their need for something firm beneath
them.
Even when he finally reached the ocean floor he recognised it
as
just one more level
and the next day he swam further before he dived.

His experience below the waves did, however, make all else
seem
hard-edged and insignificant
paradoxically painful and pointless.

The noise of desire and grasping
of self, success and certainty
shook him in ways that sometimes made him want to fold
and sometimes made him want to fight.

He felt by turn remote, righteous and redundant
at once understanding and misunderstood
caring, connected and completely apart.
For a time he gave up on words
because they reinforced the stabbing separation.

Eventually a storm blew that nonsense away
and when it ended
he heard the thought,
*We can only draw from the depths we have been to.*

The shoreline blurred in the best of ways
he realised he could dive deeply in the shallows
see the brightest of colours on dry land.
He smiled often at the horizon
and occasionally drew it inland on a wave of his choosing.

Whenever the ocean roared and breached the sea wall he ran
to greet it
spending hours staggering in the wind and spray
sometimes knocked backwards off his feet
looking up at hills and sky as water crashed
pinning him to the cobbled path
piercing his eyes.

One day
to his surprise
the shoreline disappeared completely.

The shadows changed.

The question was accepted with only the slightest of shifts,
a stone breaking the surface with barely a splash
enveloped in a heartbeat
the speed of its descent determined by its form and the current
ending somewhere unseen
displacing a fragile layer
or settling atop something more secure
- impossible to tell from the shoreline.

A moment of silence
stillness
a search flickering over eyes and skin
diving down
and then
selection made
the answer rising from the depths.

'Repetition,' the old man at 102 said, 'you can never get enough of it.' He paused briefly. 'Repetition,' he said again, 'is also a falsehood wrapped in the falsehood of time mapped in the falsehood of memory used as the building block of stories. Yet repetition is essential for testing and teaching, development, distraction and most important of all fishing.'

'Fishing?'

'Requires distance,' the old man at 102 nodded, 'and the willingness to seem stupidly forgetful. It also requires curiosity and connection and great timing and selection, sequencing and care.'

'And what do you fish for?'

'Insight.'

'And how do you fish?'

'By contracting, by dissolving all the layers that have come to fill and fatten the circle of self, until all that is left is the dot at the very centre, a dot that is a circle too, unrepeatable and unending. I told you this once in a dream. I hope you remember.' The old man's eyes glittered. 'Expansion, the casting out of something appropriate, follows contraction. This is Nature's secret. Be receptive to the response it gets.'

'What if there is no response?'

The old man chuckled. 'Try casting on the other side.'

'Are you being serious?'

The question was accepted with only the slightest of shifts;
a stone breaking the surface with barely a splash
enveloped in a heartbeat
the speed of its descent determined by its form and the
current
ending somewhere unseen
displacing a fragile layer
or settling atop something more secure
- impossible to tell from the shoreline.

A moment of silence
stillness
a search flickering over eyes and skin
diving down
and then
selection made
the answer rising from the depths.

The old man stands with his back against the corner of the bank
and watches the young mother, already athlete-fit,
steering her pram without hesitation through the early morning crowd.

He wonders if the baby can see the effects of her parent's confidence.
He thinks of the Moses story and counts silently

*100*

Further back
and losing ground to the young mother's every step
comes an elderly couple.

The man shuffles forward
pushing his scrunched-up wife
in her scratched wheelchair,
his breath raggedy
steaming in the cold winter air.

Stopping at the roadside
he keeps wheels and useless toes well back
waiting for permission.

The old man sees the lights change and counts

*101*

The fox is laying only a few feet from his front door,
its glassy eyes fish-like
its matted fur crisp and snug against the kerb,
its mouth locked open as if mid-bite.

He knows the fox by name
- its nature name
not the one given by people at the petrol station.
He knows because the fox visited often in the dead of night
and the pair danced together in the garden grass.

*The kerb is a perfect final resting place*
*for one so bold*
the old man thinks.

He smiles
as tears run down his face
and counts

*102*

‘Max, now you are a big boy, now you are five years old, tell me, what is your favourite colour?’

‘Mummy, my favourite colour is red.’

‘And what is your favourite food?’

‘My favourite food is pasta.’

‘And what is your favourite of everything?’

‘My favourite of everything is happy.’

Once I met a man who had learnt how to forget himself,
even in his dreams.

I asked him why he laughed so much.

He told me why he cried.

*************

Printed in Poland
by Amazon Fulfillment
Poland Sp. z o.o., Wrocław
17 April 2023

b99a60ba-efda-47a4-8052-80107ce78f75R01